This Book Belongs To:

____

I Prayed For A Sister

Rashad E. Lowery Jr.
Phyllis Dyson

Strength Builders Publishing LLC

Dedication

This book is dedicated to all the dreamers to never give up and know that prayer works. Also, to my amazing family, my sons, Terrell and Rashad, daughter-in-love, Jasmine, grandchildren, Rashad Jr., Isaiah, and Joy.

My name is Rashad Jr.
I love to play basketball.
I love to draw, especially
basketball courts with players
and the hoops.

I have a baby brother named
Isaiah Mark who is three years old.
My Dad and I taught him how to play
basketball. We have fun together
with our parents.

One day, I said to my Mommy and
Daddy that I wanted a baby sister
really bad. My Mommy looked
surprised and said, "Rashad,
I am not having a baby now!"

I prayed every night before
going to bed for a baby sister.
There were times when I felt that
I would never see my dream come
true but I kept on praying.

One day my parents sat me down
and said, "Rashad, your prayers
came true! You and Isaiah will be
big brothers soon to a baby sister."

I had a big smile from ear to ear!
I was so happy and said "Mommy
and Daddy, I prayed for my sister!
God did it for me!"

Each month I saw my baby sister
growing in my Mommy's tummy.

The day came when my parents
told me that my sister was ready
to come. They went to the hospital
and I was so excited that I could
not even sleep.

The day finally came! I met my
little sister while she was laid on
my Mommy's tummy. Her name was
Joy Elle Sade, and she was so
beautiful. I stood next to the bed,
filled with happiness.

After Joy came home, I was allowed
to hold her and talk to her. I told
her, "I prayed for you to be born,
Joy. I love you so much."

Joy is talking, crawling, and trying
to walk now. My parents, Isaiah,
Joy, and I have fun every day.

I remember a song that I sang
with my parents called Way Maker.
That was my prayer. A way was
made for me to become a big
brother to my little sister, Joy.

The End